Made in the USA
Middletown, DE
16 May 2022

65850827R00062